Godly
CONTENTMENT

# Godly CONTENTMENT

Fran Rogers

"But godliness with contentment is great gain."
1 Timothy 6:6

Godly
CONTENTMENT

1st Edition
© 2020 Fran Rogers
7th in Series
Little Books about the Magnitude of God
Father and Family Books

ISBN–13-978-1732681446

All rights reserved

godsgracegodsglory.com

Scripture quotations are from the Holy Bible KJV
In the public domain.

Cover Image by Heidi Viars

Acknowledgments

I continue to praise my heavenly Father for His abundant mercy and grace.

His constant revelation of the fulfillment of His promises through His Son, Jesus Christ, is His joy that keeps me close to Him.

The Holy Spirit commands the life of Christ in me to accomplish all He desires.

Family and friends are those who express their love to me as I serve our Lord.

Readers were encouragers as they supported this series on WordPress

# CONTENTS

Introduction

1. The Authority of Contentment ............................ 11
2. Born for Contentment ....................................... 15
3. The Essence of Contentment .............................. 19
4. The Image of Contentment ................................. 23
5. Contentment with God our Father ...................... 27
6. Contentment in Jesus Christ .............................. 31
7. The Reason and Season of Contentment ............. 35
8. The Center of Contentment ................................ 39
9. The Spirit of Contentment .................................. 43
10. Joy and Contentment ......................................... 47
11. The Lens of Contentment ................................... 53
12. Humility and Contentment ................................. 57
13. The Voice of Contentment .................................. 61
14. The Price of Contentment ................................... 65
15. Patience that Leads to Contentment .................... 69
16. The Flow of Contentment ................................... 73
17. Contentment vs. Anxiety .................................... 77
18. Peace and Contentment ...................................... 81
19. A Conclusive Contentment ................................. 85
From the Author ....................................................... 87

# Introduction

The Lord has led me since 2017, to continue my search for contentment ~ discovered in Him alone. It is easy to read, talk about, and search for its meaning. Like "humility," our subject for 2014, "contentment" is sought after, prayed for, desired with the whole heart, soul, mind, and strength, and more importantly, waited for with patient endurance. All of these are possible only by His working in us.

Contentment is a subject not only to be studied and pursued but described in many ways. It is the desire of most people but misunderstood when it comes to knowing how contentment is achieved.

We learn that contentment does not come from possessing the things of this world. Our first parents experienced what I call the seventh sense (we will look at this later) in the Garden of Eden. They were content until Satan convinced them they needed more than God had given. We live in the same world, but with a greater need.

Contentment is a state of being. No one is born content. The enemy supernaturally instilled the spirit of discontent and only one who is stronger than he can deliver us from it.

**Divine Contentment**

For many years Thomas Watson's book, ***The Art of Divine Contentment,*** has been a source of study and delight for me. You can download free at ccel.org or free MP3 at Still Waters Revival (puritandownloads.com.)

Jesus died to deliver us from this horrific power of oppression and discontent, which is the opposite from life in His kingdom. I called 2017 the year of contentment ~ "a movement for contentment" ~ long needed for the Christian community. What effect would our contentment have upon the world?

> **"Blessed be the God and Father of our Lord Jesus Christ, who in Christ, has blessed us with every spiritual blessing in heavenly places."** Ephesians 1:3

Gracious Father in heaven, it is you who has created us so that we may delight ourselves in you. You have redeemed us and restored us to an even greater estate from which our first parents fell. Only you can bring us from the power of the oppressor to you, to know your presence and power, to work in us supernaturally this contentment for which you saved us in Christ. Draw us by the power of your Holy Spirit. Open our hearts, our minds, our ears, our wills, to you, to our Lord Jesus Christ and your Holy Spirit, so that we do not miss anything you have **prepared for us. In Jesus'** name, I pray. Amen.

# 1

# The Authority of Contentment

**"You shall be holy, for I am holy."**
**1 Peter 1:16**

Why is contentment so rare in human creatures? It seems that the status quo, even for God's children, is brokenness. This condition is becoming more and more acceptable as a means of relating to others.

Most would agree that we live in a world of oppression. The world is not a desirable place to be, but we, as God's people, have a directive. God set the mandate for us before time began (Ephesians 1:4). I heard recently, "We are a distinctive people." But this is not a new statement. It is the Biblical perspective for the Christian church.

God, our heavenly Father, is the authority of His kingdom. He rules in holiness, in love, and grace in the lives of His people. By His power, He has birthed a family for Himself, growing us and conforming us to the image of Jesus Christ, His Son, who is "the first of many brethren" (Romans 8:29).

He came, in Jesus, to work in us a new life, compatible with Himself. He is teaching us what His kingdom is, training us for eternity with Him and by His Word we know what He expects to do in us. We will look at four of these points in this chapter ~ those that begin with what we are to "BE."

We begin this treatise by describing contentment as a supernatural state of "being." I will add here that it is part of the legacy of God's kingdom.
Being a "joint-heir" with Christ has many facets. Each one is from the same source of God's grace. The authority that commands us to "BE" is the source that works what God requires in every part. All characteristics of the Christian life are distinctive in that they are beyond our natural abilities. Andrew Murray states in *Waiting on God*, "what He commands is a promise of what He will do."

We will look at His commands to "be holy," "be glad," "be still," and "be content." We will see how contentment fits and flows from holiness, gladness, and stillness, and why He commands these for His people.

### "Be Holy"

We begin in the Old Testament in Leviticus to see God's separation of a people for Himself, then in the New Testament the repetition in 1 Peter to those who are separated and made holy in Christ.

In Leviticus 11:44-45 and Leviticus 20:7, we see that He brought the Israelites out of bondage. He separated them from the land of Egypt, "to be your God. You shall, therefore, be holy, for I am holy." He is holy and makes His people holy.

In 1 Peter 1:13-16, he quotes the same command to God's people in our day. This section of Peter's letter is titled, "Called to be holy."

Please read this part of his letter to the Jewish Christians. What I find interesting in both the Old and New covenants

# The Authority of Contentment

is the statement, "You **shall be** holy." In agreement, we consecrate ourselves, with the mind-set that He will do the work in us. (See also 1 Peter 3:15)

## "Be Glad"
Psalm 32:11 is the last verse of this Psalm that begins with the word "Blessed." I will not take away from your gladness by telling you what is in this Psalm. If you are serious about living a contented life, you must read Psalm 32 for yourself.

Reading the whole Psalm gives us insight into why we are to "be glad." I would suggest reading it every day for a month and see what happens. Perhaps you will establish The Glad Rule in your home.

## "Be Still"
Psalm 32 and Psalm 46 are short Psalms but packed with the context from which we find memorable verses.

Psalm 46 begins with, "God is our refuge and strength, a very present help in times of trouble." Reading this Psalm through verse 10 gives us an understanding of why He instructs us to "Be still."

## "Be Content"
If we have done our homework through the first three subjects of "BEing," we will come to a better understanding of this distinction of contentment. The writer of Hebrews 13:5, like Peter, quotes from the Old Testament (Joshua 1:5).

> **"Keep your life free from love of money, and be content with what you have, for he has said, "I will never leave you nor forsake you."**

From the first statement of God's authority in our contentment, "I am your God" to "I will never leave you nor forsake you," we have the reason for our contentment. When we know Him, He will be our contentment, here and for eternity. Contentment is wrapped up in His written word and His Living Word, Jesus Christ, as He works it in us.

Three things we need to remember to carry us through this treatise:

>1. Godly contentment is supernatural, possible only for God's people.
>2. It is the result of a relationship between God, our heavenly Father, and His children.
>3. He will teach and show us what He is doing in us.

Training for the Christian is a life-long process that fits us for heaven and eternity with our heavenly Father and our Lord Jesus Christ. This world is not just a wilderness, and a battleground of brokenness, but the place where our heavenly Father proves His authorship, power, victory, and majesty through the lives of His people.

Gracious Father, we praise you that you have chosen a people to be holy unto you, a distinctive family that you are training to be your image-bearers. Fill us with your Holy Spirit to do the work that you promise and command in us as your children. Give the world the unique image of your kingdom as we love and reach out with the gospel of our Lord Jesus Christ to those who are in adversity. In His name, I pray. Amen.

# 2

# Born for Contentment

**"Which were born, not of blood, nor of the will of the flesh, nor of the will of man, but of God."**
**John 1:13**

Everyone who comes into this world is "born for adversity" (Proverbs 17:17). God's children are "born again" for contentment.

Years ago, when Ansley, our oldest granddaughter, started elementary school, I asked her why children go to school. Her reply was, "So that we can get a job, make money, and buy what we want." She was learning well at an early age what the world teaches about contentment. Now, at the age of twenty-seven, she is married, has a stepson, a five-year-old daughter, and a two-week-old son. She and her husband lost their month-old baby girl in 2018 and had a miscarriage in 2019. Through adversity, she is learning to be content with what she has.

In this world of oppression, we are taught that we have the power to accomplish whatever makes us happy. This is not the contentment for which God's people are born. Let's leave behind the fallacy that we are responsible for our state of being.

True contentment ~ godly contentment ~ comes to us by the supernatural power of God, our heavenly Father. He desired us and sired us for His pleasure and contentment. Just as we learn from infancy how to survive physically, we must learn, at His feet, how to be content in this world.

**Desire to Desire What God Desires**
Let us recall the apostle Paul's words, "I have learned….to be content." (Philippians 4:11) What God gives us in our new birth is "a new heart, and a new spirit" (Ezekiel 36:26) with a desire for that which is eternal.

Learning about true contentment is not easy. It is as foreign to humanity as anything we can study or desire. It is beyond imagination, so supernatural that we cannot think about it without being overwhelmed. We are reminded of Jesus' promise, "Whoever drinks of the water that I will give him will never be thirsty again. The water that I will give him will become in him a spring of water welling up to eternal life." (John 4:14)

Eternal life becomes a fountain (Psalm 36:9), a stream (Isaiah 35:6), then breaks forth into rivers of living water (John 7:37-39). The source is God, Himself, through Christ, His Son, and the power of the Holy Spirit working in the heart to produce His own life. Is this what He meant when He said, "The kingdom of God is within you?" Luke 17:21

The new birth is the spring. Growing by the grace and knowledge of our Lord Jesus Christ brings the blessings of His presence and power, blessings we cannot fathom, or control, at times, carrying us away with the flow.

**Oppression ~~~~ Adversity ~~~~ Contentment**
The contentment of God's children is the opposite end of the spectrum from oppression, as far as heaven is from the earth. Between oppression and contentment, the reality of

adversity remains part of every person's life. **Contentment is God's blessing and His gift of grace, that His children may live content in Christ, in the middle of adversity. It is more than just having what we think we need but receiving what He has so graciously prepared for us ~ more than we could ask or think.** (1 Corinthians 2:9; Ephesians 3:20)

As we continue to proclaim the legacy of God's kingdom, we will share what He is teaching us of this supernatural, phenomenal gift of His contentment.

Dear Father in heaven, many ask why you allow oppression and adversity. Keep us close to you as you are teaching us your thoughts and your ways concerning your kingdom here on earth. We praise you for contentment that is ours in Christ, and the legacy that is ours as joint-heirs with Him now and for eternity. Show us your ways O Lord; teach us your paths; lead us in your truth and teach us. For Thou art the God of our salvation. On Thee do we wait all the day. In Jesus' name, I pray. Amen.

# 3

# The Essence of Contentment

**"The water that I shall give him shall be in him
a well of water springing up into everlasting life.
John 4:14.**

The essence of contentment is distilled from the presence of the heavenly Father in His children. It is a seventh sense that comes from the new birth. God's Spirit within us springs up to eternal life in the new heart and spirit directing our course of living, preparing us for the eternal glory with the Father and His Son. Most of us have something of our parents' reflections ~ some trait or expression. The same is true of our relationship with our heavenly Father, who, in Christ, reveals Himself. We, as His children, exhibit His character, when by His Spirit and His written Word, He conforms us more and more to His image. He is content to have desired us and sired us for His own family.

We are continuing to learn and proclaim the legacy of God's kingdom through our books and our blog, *God's Grace ~ God's Glory*. We are each given short-term goals, but none of us have arrived at His planned destination.

We are learning to live in this wilderness of oppression, trusting His Word, His presence, and His power with us (Ephesians 3:20-21).

## The Sixth Sense

We are born into this world with five senses. I believe that "faith" is a sixth sense that comes with the new birth.

Regeneration brings us in faith and repentance to citizenship in God's kingdom. Faith brings a sense of distinction from the old life. Although it is a new sense, it is relative to the other five senses.

Faith comes by hearing the gospel, the good news of Christ and our redemption (Romans 10:17). We read God's Word, and the Holy Spirit moves with our spirit, so we know that we are God's children (Romans 10:17, Ephesians 1:18). We touch and hold His Word as He teaches us (Proverbs 4:13; 1 Timothy 4:16; Philippians 2: 14-16). We "taste and see that the Lord is good" (Psalm 34:8; Matthew 4:4). We become a sweet fragrance of Christ (2 Corinthians 2:15). These are but samples of how God uses the senses He created in us to birth us to a living hope and the inheritance that we have as joint-heirs with Christ. (1 Peter 1:3-4)

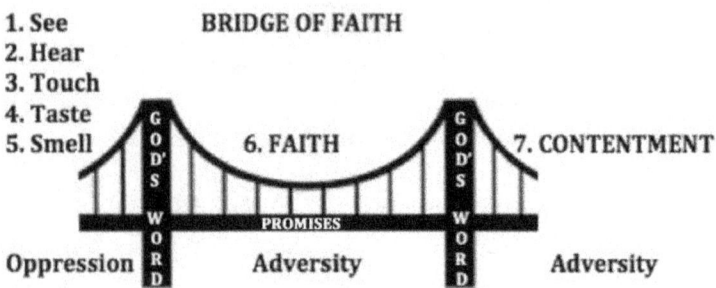

**Faith Leads to Contentment**
Faith affects our senses as we grow in grace and knowledge of our Lord Jesus *Christ* (2 Peter 3:18; Romans 8:28-29).

Faith becomes the bridge, the means to the whole of God's kingdom. Here is where we connect faith and contentment, contentment being the seventh and complete sense in communion with the Father.

Our Father uses faith to bring us out of the state of oppression through adversity. We would rather say that His presence and power lift us above the adversity and brings us to the state of contentment. We do not escape adversity, but in it, we learn to live in conformity to the image of Christ. His Word and faith in His Word train our senses. By these, we accept and live unmoved by our circumstances. We practice keeping our focus on God, our Father, and our hearts centered in Christ and His promises, as the Holy Spirit leads us.


Dear Father, thank you for filling us with your fulness and spreading your love in our hearts; for becoming life to us through your Son, Jesus Christ, our Savior, and Lord. Continue to fill us with your Holy Spirit, and to work your contentment in us. In Jesus' name, I pray. **Amen.**

# 4

# The Image of Contentment

**"And God said, Let us make man in our image, after our likeness:"
Genesis 1:26a**

Let's review the main points of godly contentment.

1. Godly Contentment is supernatural, possible only for God's people.
2. It is the result of a relationship between God, our heavenly Father, and His children.
3. He will teach and show us what He is doing in us.

In this chapter, we want to meditate on God's Word and what we learn from Him concerning His image and how He works His image in us as His children. He is content with His work in and through us. Therefore, we must learn to be content with what He is doing. From the beginning, He saw that everything He had made was "good."

**"And God said, Let us make man in our <u>image</u>, after our <u>likeness</u>:"** Genesis 1:26a

He is still working all things for our good and conforming us to the image of His Son.

> "And we know that all things work together for good to them that love God, to them who are the called according to his purpose. For whom he did foreknow, he also did predestinate to be conformed to the image of his Son, that he might be the firstborn among many brethren." Romans 8:28-29

We are transformed into the image of the Lord as we continue to look to Him for all things.

> "And we all, with unveiled face, beholding the glory of the Lord, are being transformed into the same image from one degree of glory to another. For this comes from the Lord who is the Spirit." 2 Corinthians 3:18

The apostle John and the Psalmist speak of the future when we see God in all His glory.

> "Beloved, now we are children of God, and it has not appeared as yet what we will be. We know that when He appears, we will be like Him, because we will see Him just as He is." 1 John 3:2

> "As for me, I shall behold your face in righteousness; when I awake, I shall be satisfied with your likeness."
> Psalm 17:15

# The Image of Contentment

While we wait for His second coming, we can be content in our role as a servant, even as He served while He was here.

> "**It is enough** for the disciple that he be **as his master**, and the servant **as his Lord**." Matthew 10:25

Dear Father, you have created us in your image, and given us new hearts that you may fill us with your Spirit and conform us to the image of your Son. It is enough for us to be like our Master, and one day, to behold your face in righteousness and be satisfied with your likeness. Make us content in the work you are doing in us now, by your grace and for your glory. In Jesus' name, I pray. Amen.

# 5

# Contentment with God our Father

**"See what kind of love the Father has given to us, that we should be called children of God; and so we are. The reason why the world does not know us is that it did not know him."**
**1 John 3:1**

As I sat in contemplation, praying how to start this chapter, I realized that we, as children of the Kingdom of God, begin everything with GOD. My thoughts, my words, my actions all play off the truth that only our heavenly Father can teach us. I have always taught, especially my grandchildren, for fourteen summers, from the premise, "In the beginning, GOD." Add to this, the first petition in the Lord's Prayer, "Our Father …. Hallowed be Thy name," In these, we know where to start thinking. From these, we witness to others who we are and what we believe.

His teaching never changes because He never changes. "The world lies in wickedness" (1 John 5:19) "under the power of the evil one" (ESV). And we, as His children, are prone to forget that He leads us in "the paths of righteousness for His name's sake" (Psalm 23:3).

In the power of His light, He leads His people through the darkness of this world. From start to finish, it is and always will be God, our Father, at the helm.

### Knowing Him

The difference is in how we relate to Him. GOD, to some people, is nothing; purely speculation. He may pass as a thought through the minds of others. But in His kingdom, we relate to God as our Father. There is a vast, magnitudinal difference in the minds, hearts, and lives of those who know Him as FATHER. The keyword here is "know."

"Knowing" in God's Word denotes intimacy, being close enough to live in assurance, without a doubt, with the one we know. A child who lives with a father who cares, promises, and fulfills his promises, can live content. We are living "with" God, our Father. He is not just a supernatural being that has "set His throne above the heavens…His kingdom ruling over all" (Psalm 103:19). He is transcendent, encompassing all, but He is also, supernaturally, living in our hearts, our minds, and our strength.

He is always with us. He is GOD to His children when He is nothing to others. He is caring for us in the smallest detail and the higher things. While the world lives in despair and hopelessness, He supplies every need, whether physical or spiritual. We must know, trust, and live in light of these truths, and set our minds on Him as GOD, in prayer and meditation on His Word.

By His power working in us, He is able, "exceeding abundantly able" to "hold us by the hand and guide us with His counsel" to know Him as Father beyond what we can ask or think of Him (Ephesians 3:20-21; Psalm 73:23-24).

## His Goal for His Children

*GOD Is Our Goal ~ GOD'S Plan for His People* published in 2017, is a summary of what I taught my grandchildren and relates to God's goal for us as His children. He, in His purpose for our creation and redemption before the beginning of time, planned how He would bring us through this wilderness to Himself. He has not, and will not fail, to be GOD and Father to us.

Has He ever failed in His promises? Are we content with Him as our God and Father? What more does He need to do for us? Let us draw near to Him; stay close to Him, and we will, through all our trials and temptations, learn to be content with Him and all He has planned for us.

Gracious Father in heaven, you teach us in your Word what you want us to know about you. By your Spirit of Christ working in us, you bring us to yourself so that you may fill our minds and hearts with your love and grace. You are a Father like no other, who provides all we need for this life and eternity. Send your Holy Spirit today; mark us as your own that we may be witnesses of your promises and the fulfillment in us of all that you have prepared for us. Make us know you as Father in the middle of a world that does not hold this role sacred—a world that lives in the state of oppression. Thank you for leading us to keep our minds on you, no matter the circumstances. In Jesus' name, I pray. Amen.

# 6

# Contentment in Jesus Christ

**"Come to me, all ye that labor and are heavy-laden and I will give you rest."
Matthew 11:28**

I was writing this chapter at 6:24; awake since 3:34 with thoughts of all the things I had planned for the week, in addition to the everyday work I have to do: doctors' appointments and last-minute details for publishing our next book.

I was writing a letter for our two-year-old great-granddaughter on the occasion of her dedication next Lord's Day, and keeping a watch on and dressing the diabetic ulcer on Jerry's foot, etc. First and last, most things are my duty as Jerry's caregiver. Yet, God has provided His grace for the other things He has predestined for us, all to His glory.

How do we do all He has planned without sinking in despair?

God, our Father, was content before the foundation of the world with His Son, Jesus Christ. They were content, together, in making a covenant for Jesus to come to us, to live a perfect life for us, to give His life for us for our salvation. They are content now with what they have done and what they are doing continually for us and in us by the Holy Spirit.

### The Course and the Source
That morning as I looked at my two full plates, I saw Jesus as the main course for that week and every week. We plan everything around Him. He is the physician. He is the reason for writing a letter to my great-granddaughter. He is the source of contentment in the middle of what could be confusion and frustration.

When things seem hectic, the Father says, "Listen to my Son" (Matthew 17:5 ESV)

He is the Shepherd, keeping and leading His sheep in the way we are to go. In time, we learn that when we get ahead of Him, He may sometimes let us go until our impatient steam runs out. Then, we must wait for Him to renew, refresh, and restore us in Christ before we continue with joy and contentment in Him. At other times, He holds us back and keeps us close until He leads us out on the path He has chosen for the moment and the day.

Some of God's children live under the control of the oppressive spirit of this world. It doesn't have to be this way.

The Father has given us His Son.

Jesus has given us Himself for a life of contentment now and forever. They have given us the Holy Spirit to finish the work He planned before the foundation of the world.

Gracious Father in heaven, we thank you for granting us all things that pertain to life and godliness through Jesus Christ, your Son. Draw us today to Him; in Him, keep us close to you, by your Spirit, leading us to fulfill all that you have planned for us. Let our contentment be in Him alone. In Jesus' name, I pray. Amen.

# 7

# The Reason and Season for Contentment

**"To whom God would make known what are the riches of the glory of this mystery among the Gentiles; which is Christ in you, the hope of glory:"
Colossians 1:27**

Jesus is the reason and the season for contentment. We cannot say this strongly enough. We looked at the role of God, our Father. We will look soon at the role of the Holy Spirit.

Why are we centering on Jesus, the second person of the Trinity? There are many reasons.

Our last chapter on Jesus would not be enough. Remember John's last statement of his gospel, "the world itself could not contain the books that would be written." So, if you want to be more productive and content with what God has prepared for us as His children, don't skim this chapter but stay with me to hear what He wants us to know.

With a Christian worldview, we see through the eyes of the church ~ the body of Christ. He is the head, and we are growing up into Him as we continue in His Word. We are set free from the bondage of ignorance, the power of death and sin, of fear, and the world's influence. How is this possible without Jesus Christ? We would still be in our sin and the chaotic upheaval of the world.

At the precise time God planned, Jesus was born into this world to fulfill the promises God had made. (Galatians 4:4-7)

Why are Jesus' followers not rioting, and complaining? Jesus makes the difference.

## How the Triune God Works His Plan and Power on Earth

Let's look at how His plan is established in Jesus His Son. God, the Father, sent His Son to make the difference ~ between the world and His kingdom ~ a kingdom of righteousness, peace, and joy.

Jesus lived a perfect life of righteousness under the law, fulfilling every jot and tittle. His life is the central point of God's plan. Through his death and resurrection, we receive His life (1 Peter 1:3). Since His ascension, He is ruling at the right hand of the Father on our behalf. He is leading those who are His to live in union with Him. He is giving us a new life, a supernatural life, in a new relationship with Him and the Father. The Holy Spirit is working all things according to His will and covenant with His people.

## The Trinity

Let's look more closely: God, the Father + God, the Son + God, the Spirit = The Trinity. Take away God, the Son ~ We would not know God the Father, nor would the Holy Spirit have been sent to us.

From the Biblical references, we see how the Father focuses all things on His Son. We understand that the whole of God's Word, from beginning to end, is about Jesus Christ, the promised, living, dying, living, ruling, and reigning Messiah.

# The Reason and Season for Contentment

**He is the First and the Last, the Alpha and Omega.**
We do not have room or time to include all references to Christ, but only a few that relate to His role, His relationship to the Father, the Holy Spirit, and us.

The first promise of the Messiah, Conqueror, and Savior ~ Genesis 3:15; the promise of a Son ~ Isaiah 7:14; Matthew 1:23

> He is the image of the invisible God ~ "**for by Him were all things created, in heaven and on earth**, visible and invisible, whether thrones or dominions or rulers or authorities - **all things were created through him and for him**. And He is before all things, and in him, all things hold together." Colossians 1:15-20

> "Making known to us the mystery of his will, according to his purpose, which he set forth in Christ as a plan for the fullness of time, **to unite all things in him**, things in heaven and things on earth." Ephesians 1:9-10

John, the Baptist's witness of the Son: Matthew 3:11
The Father's witness of His Son:
Matthew 3:17; 11:27; 17:5; 1 John 5:6-12;
John 17:1-7, 24;
The Holy Spirit's witness of the Son: John 14:26; John 15;26; John 16:7, 12-15

> "He will glorify me, for he will take what is mine and declare it to you. All that the Father has is mine;

therefore I said that he will take what is mine and declare it to you." John 16:14-15

We have only scratched the surface. There are layers, "precept upon precept" of "the way, the truth, and the life" that is ours in Jesus Christ, our Lord. All we need for life, godliness, and contentment are combined into this one "person" and beyond us, to discover what is ours in Him. He is the center and root of all things blessed, beautiful, filling, and overflowing with the goodness and grace for all that we need.

All that is precious, amazing, and fathomless is promised in Him, revealed and fulfilled in those who are His children.

### The Season for Contentment
Because Jesus Christ holds the secret, the means, and the power in all things for contentment, we must continue to keep our eyes, ears, and all our senses on Him. He is the reason for our contentment. Therefore, the season for our contentment in Him is year-round, never-ending, now and forever.

Gracious Father, we thank you for your plan for life, in and through Jesus Christ. He is to us wisdom, righteousness, sanctification, and redemption, who upholds all things by the word of His power, who sits at your right hand, ruling and reigning until you have put all things under His feet. We praise you that your greatness is unsearchable. Thank you for this unspeakable gift of grace and life in Him, for now and eternity. Open our eyes to see and live in the wonder of Christ to and in us as your people. In Jesus' name, I pray. Amen.

# 8

# The Center of Contentment

### "It is finished." John 19:30

Why do I keep harping on Jesus Christ as relating to contentment? When He said, "It is finished," He not only spoke of the beginning and the end but more importantly, of what was central. He had lived His life in full obedience to the law, which no one else could do, and according to the prophecies, He had submitted His life as the sacrifice the Father required for our sin. In the end, He had prepared and was leaving for His people the means for the abundant life He promised His disciples. Those who are "in Christ" ~ born again to a living hope by His resurrection (1 Peter 1:3) have this eternal hope. This truth outweighs anything the world has to offer. This life and hope glories in, and is supplied by, the very life of Christ, Himself.

He has given us His Spirit, His mind, His words, and His life (John 6:63). To live for us and give His life for us was not just a flippant desire, hoping that some would believe and consult His teaching.

All God planned was accomplished through Jesus' life, death, and resurrection, revealed and fulfilled by the power of His Holy Spirit.

To have a little of Jesus is to negate His suffering and sacrifice for us. To consult Him only when things are rough in this life is to live on crumbs from the Master's table. He has promised to be all things to His people ~ not to the world ~ but to His people.

He died to sanctify us in Himself (John 17:19; Ephesians 5:25-27; Hebrews 2:11).

When we say, "The Lord is my Shepherd, I shall not want," we are echoing His truth and our contentment in Him. We want nothing but what He wants for us.

**What Else Do We Need?**
God, our Father, has provided all things in Christ for His people (Romans 8:32; 2 Peter 1:3). As the Galatians were pressured to be circumcised, some today want to add to Christ when Christ is enough for this life and the next.

We do not need practices from other religions. I tried Transcendental Meditation years ago. It was useful for all I wanted it to do, but Christ soon won over this practice. TM had to go; I did not want to be my own god. There are many religions. Christ is not a religion but a living person. His people do not worship Him in a manger or on a cross. What He came to do is done, "finished" ~ ended. He now sits at the right hand of God the Father, ruling and reigning, with all authority and power.

He is our High Priest, interceding, intervening for us. He is our Prophet, through His Spirit and His written Word, to direct us. He is our King, ruling, hearing, and seeing our trials and struggles through the wilderness of this life. We have His promised power and presence with us so that we can rejoice in Him always, no matter the circumstances.

*When Morning Gilds the Skies*

When morning gilds the skies, my heart awaking cries.
May Jesus Christ be praised.
Alike at work and prayer to Jesus, I repair,
May Jesus Christ be praised.

When sleep her balm denies, my silent spirit sighs;
May Jesus Christ be praised.
When evil thoughts molest,
with this I shield my breasts;
May Jesus Christ be praised.

Does sadness fill my mind? A solace here I find;
May Jesus Christ be praised.
Or fades my earthly bliss? My comfort still is this.
May Jesus Christ be praised.
*Edward Caswall* (1814-1878)

Dear Father, bring us as your people to see, know, love, obey and rejoice in you today. Let the world see Christ in us. In Jesus' name, I pray. Amen.

# 9

# The Spirit of Contentment

**"Hereby know we that we dwell in him, and he in us, because he hath given us of his Spirit."**
**1 John 4:13**

As we begin this chapter, we want to remember the three main truths that pertain to contentment.

1. Godly contentment is supernatural, possible only for God's people.
2. It is the result of a relationship between God and His children.
3. He will teach and show us what He is doing in us.

From the first point, we consider contentment to be of a different realm than the natural. It is a divine working of God's kingdom here on earth as He is preparing us for eternity with Him. The person and work of His Son, Jesus Christ, show and establish the Father's will for our contentment. It is a relationship brought about by the revelation and fulfillment of the power of His Holy Spirit.

We have looked at *Contentment with God Our Father, Contentment in Jesus Christ, The Reason and Season for Contentment, and The Center of Contentment*, all relating to the expectation and anticipation of contentment in this life.

Again, all is based, not on our working, but on the promises of God's Word as revealed and fulfilled by the Holy Spirit (2 Peter 1:19-21).

## The Power of the Holy Spirit

Let's think of the power of the Holy Spirit that makes what the Father willed, and the Son accomplished for us a reality.

How did we come to hear and to know God? How did we first believe?

How do we continue to believe when others scoff and ridicule the truths of God's Word and His kingdom?

How can we be content in this life without what the world offers?

How do we continue to grow in grace and knowledge of Jesus Christ, seeking the kingdom of God and His righteousness, while others are looking for happiness and contentment in material possessions or human relationships?

## A Mindset of the New Birth

This contentment is a heavenly mindset of those who have been born of the Spirit (John 3:3-8).

> "There is therefore now no condemnation for those who are in Christ Jesus.
> For the law of the Spirit of life has set you free in Christ Jesus from the law of sin and death."
> Romans 8:1-2

The Holy Spirit is the Spirit of Christ, His life by the power of His Spirit in us.

> "What no eye has seen, nor ear heard, nor the heart of man imagined, what God has prepared for those who love him"—these things God has revealed to us through the Spirit.

For the Spirit searches everything, even the depths of God. (See 2 Corinthians 6-16)

From the beginning of time, the Holy Spirit has been bringing light into our darkness. He is continually revealing the will and the work of the Father in His children.

The Spirit of contentment is the same as the power that raised Jesus from the dead, the same power that "made alive in Christ" those who were dead in trespasses and sin (Ephesians 2:1-5).
Paul prayed for the early Christians to know of their inheritance in Christ;

> "and what is the immeasurable greatness of his power toward us who believe, according to the working of his great might that he worked in Christ when he raised him from the dead and seated him at his right hand in the heavenly places," Ephesians 1:19-20

> "that according to the riches of his glory he may grant you to be strengthened with power through his Spirit in your inner being," Ephesians 3:16

**The Father, the Son, and the Holy Spirit's Working**
In many of Paul's letters, He speaks of the three persons of the God-head.

> "being strengthened with all power, according to his glorious might, for all endurance and patience with joy; giving thanks to the Father, who has qualified you to share in the inheritance of the saints in light. He has delivered us from the domain of darkness and

transferred us to the kingdom of his beloved Son, in whom we have redemption, the forgiveness of sins." Colossians 1:11-14

## The Things of the Spirit

"For those who live according to the flesh set their minds on the things of the flesh, but those who live according to the Spirit set their minds on the things of the Spirit. For to set the mind on the flesh is death, but to set the mind on the Spirit is life and peace." Romans 8:5-6

We are redeemed by the blood of Christ so that our body is the temple of His Holy Spirit (1 Corinthians 6:19-20).

"And those who belong to Christ Jesus have crucified the flesh with its passions and desires." Galatians 5:24

Contentment is for those who are "led by the Spirit" (Galatians 5:18); "walk by the Spirit" (Galatians 5:16) and for those who "live by the Spirit" (Galatians 5:25). Who is not content who bears the fruit of the Spirit (Galatians 5:22-23)?

Dear Gracious and Holy Father, we thank you and praise you for your work of love and compassion ~ restoring us to a right relationship with you and freedom in Christ that brings contentment. Enable us to crucify the desires of the flesh that we may bear the fruit of the Spirit of Christ. In Jesus' name, I pray. Amen.

# 10

# Joy and Contentment

**"and your joy no man taketh from you."**
**John 16:22**

How can I experience joy and contentment during these grueling times? How do I write about joy and contentment in the middle of uncertainty? I don't know how, but I must. It is part of our work for Christ and His kingdom. It is during these times that He proves His joy in us.

He teaches and works His will in us by the power of His Holy Spirit. We live, not according to our circumstances, but by our focus upon Him and His calling on our lives. There would never be real joy or contentment if we did not know Him, but Christ in us is the reason for our joy and contentment, no matter how difficult our days.

In 2017 the Lord chose to prove an even greater working than before ~ with more trials. Without them, we would never know how precious and powerful His presence is with us. His Word is not only "powerful and active" (Hebrews 4:12) but also filling and fruitful in the worst of times.

From these thoughts, we venture to share what His Word says about joy. Please take the time to read and meditate on these truths and let them settle in your heart. His Word is truly a lamp to our feet and a light to our path of joy through this wilderness. It is His joy that keeps us content even through the worst of times.

We started this treatise stating that all contentment is a gift from God and His Spirit working in us. Joy begins with Him, as with all that describes His kingdom and our relationship with Him. He rejoices over us with joy.

> "The Lord thy God in the midst of thee is mighty; he will save, he will rejoice over thee with joy; he will rest in his love, he will joy over thee with singing." Zephaniah 3:17

Even as He initiates joy, there is no pure joy apart from Him. Our joy is in Him.

> "..neither be ye grieved; for the joy of the Lord is your strength." Nehemiah 8:10

> "The meek also shall increase their joy in the Lord, and the poor among men shall rejoice in the Holy One of Israel." Isaiah 29:19

Jesus speaks of the "good and faithful servant: who will enter into the joy of thy lord." Matthew 25:21

> "Then will I go unto the altar of God, unto God my exceeding joy." Psalm 43:4

"for the Lord had made them joyful." (Ezra 6:22).

"Let Israel rejoice in him that made him: let the children of Zion be joyful in their King." Psalm 149:2

**Joy in Our Salvation**

"I will greatly rejoice in the Lord; my soul shall be joyful in my God; for he hath clothed me with the garments of salvation, he hath covered me with the robe of righteousness, as a bridegroom decketh himself with ornaments, and as a bride adorneth herself with her jewels." Isaiah 61:10

We have joy in God "through our Lord Jesus Christ, by whom we have now received the atonement." Romans 5:11

"Yet I will rejoice in the Lord. I will joy in the God of my salvation." Habakkuk 3:18

"And my soul shall be joyful in the Lord: it shall rejoice in his salvation." Psalm 35:9

**Joy of the Holy Ghost**

Joy is the fruit of the Spirit (Galatians 5:22).

"And ye became followers of us, and of the Lord, having received the word in much affliction, with joy of the Holy Ghost." 1 Thessalonians 1:6

> "For the kingdom of God is not meat and drink; but righteousness, and peace, and joy in the Holy Ghost." Romans 14:17

The God of hope fill you with all joy and peace through the power of the Holy Ghost (Romans 15:13).

## The Joy of Christ is a Full Joy

> "These things have I spoken unto you, that my joy might remain in you, and that your joy might be full." John 15:11

> "And ye now therefore have sorrow: but I will see you again, and your heart shall rejoice, and your joy no man taketh from you." John 16:22

> "And now come I to thee; and these things I speak in the world, that they might have my joy fulfilled in themselves." John 17:13

> "Looking unto Jesus the author and finisher of our faith; who for the joy that was set before him endured the cross, despising the shame, and is set down at the right hand of the throne of God." Hebrews 12:2

## Joy Through God's Word

> "Thy Word was unto me the joy and rejoicing of mine heart: Jeremiah 15:16

# Joy and Contentment

Paul's joy would not be abated during his last days of persecution, but it would carry him through the remainder of His ministry for the gospel.

> "But none of these things move me, neither count I my life dear unto myself, so that I might finish my course with joy, and the ministry, which I have received of the Lord Jesus, to testify the gospel of the grace of God." Acts 20:24

## Suffering and Temptation

> "To appoint unto them that mourn in Zion, to give unto them beauty for ashes, the oil of joy for mourning, the garment of praise for the spirit of heaviness; that they might be called trees of righteousness, the planting of the Lord, that he might be glorified." Isaiah 61:3

Paul spoke of "exceeding joy in tribulation" (2 Corinthians 7:4). He prayed for the Colossian church to be "Strengthened with all might, according to his glorious power, unto all patience and longsuffering with joyfulness;" Colossians 1:11

Simon Peter wrote, "But rejoice, inasmuch as ye are partakers of Christ's sufferings; that, when his glory shall be revealed, ye may be glad also with exceeding joy." 1 Peter 4:13

James wrote about "joy through various trials" (James 1:2).

## Our Joy Is an Unspeakable, Everlasting, and Exceeding Joy

> "Whom having not seen, ye love; in whom, though now ye see him not, yet believing, ye rejoice with joy unspeakable and full of glory:" 1 Peter 1:8

> "Therefore the redeemed of the Lord shall return, and come with singing unto Zion; and everlasting joy shall be upon their head: they shall obtain gladness and joy; and sorrow and mourning shall flee away." Isaiah 51:11

> "Now unto him that is able to keep you from falling, and to present you faultless before the presence of his glory with exceeding joy," Jude 1:24

Dear Heavenly Father, we thank you and praise you for your joy that is ours through your Son, Jesus Christ. Fill us more and more with your Spirit of joy that cannot be taken from us, no matter the circumstances of this life. Enable us to meditate on your Word, to hide your Word and your joy in our hearts. Help us live content within your Word, your promises, and the great salvation that is ours for eternity. In Jesus' name, I pray. Amen.

# 11

# The Lens of Contentment

**"Looking unto Jesus the author and finisher of our faith; who for the joy that was set before him endured the cross, despising the shame, and is set down at the right hand of the throne of God."**
**Hebrews 12:2**

Most people see contentment as it relates to good health, relationships, possessions, fashions, the cars we drive and the homes in which we live ~ many of these indicating a measure of success.

God gives His people a means of seeing what is different from the world. The new heart and new spirit (Ezekiel 36:26; John 3:3) given by God our Father, come with a lens that changes our focus from the world and our dependence on what we can achieve. Our view is upward, brought to see Him as the giver and supplier of all that we need. We see beyond the world's offerings to the special blessings that are ours through His Son, Jesus Christ.

The writer of the book of Hebrews leaves an appeal to God's people in the last chapter:

> "Keep your life free from the love of money." Hebrews 13:5 ESV

The world trains our children to seek contentment through what money can buy. We are trained as followers of Christ to "be content with what we have."

Why can we be content with less than what the world offers?

> ~ "for He has said, 'I will never leave you nor forsake you.'" (13:5)

The giver of all things is more precious than all the money we could accrue in this world. His presence is more significant than any relationship, entertainment, or possession offered in this generation.

His love and grace are of more value than anything. His blessings are infinite and eternally ours, while the temporal things of this world will either be lost or fade away. Nothing of this world can compare to what we experience in His supply of all things.

> "His divine power has granted to us all things that pertain to life and godliness, through the knowledge of him who called us to his own glory and excellence, by which he has granted to us his precious and very great promises, so that through them you may become partakers of the divine nature, having escaped from the corruption that is in the world because of sinful desire." 2 Peter 1:3-4

# The Lens of Contentment

Many have suffered physically and financially in attempting to keep up with higher expectations than they are able. When they learn of life in Christ, they can let go of the world's offerings and enjoy Him and what He gives.

> "But, as it is written, What no eye has seen, nor ear heard, nor the heart of man imagined, what God has prepared for those who love him"—these things God has revealed to us through the Spirit.
> Now we have received not the spirit of the world, but the Spirit who is from God, that we might understand the things freely given us by God."
> 1 Corinthians 2:9-12

Paul said, "I have learned in whatever situation I am to be content" (Philippians 4:11). He endured persecution., at the same time. rejoicing and praising the Lord because He had experienced the presence and power of God.

In His calling, devotion, and service, Paul was given "visions and revelations" (2 Corinthians 12:1). As an evangelist/tentmaker, he knew our God "who supplies all our needs" (Philippians 4:19). Paul lived with a "thorn in the flesh" ~ "the buffeting of Satan" from the religious leaders (2 Corinthians 12:7).

He could live the last part of his life in prison content with the Lord's calling and promises of the gospel. Oh, that we might say as he did, "Indeed, I count everything as loss because of the surpassing worth of knowing Christ Jesus my Lord." (Philippians 3:8)

Gracious heavenly Father, creator, and supplier of all things, open our eyes, turn them upward to see heaven opened as you pour out all that you have prepared for us in and through Jesus, our Lord. Let the world see our contentment with you and all that you desire for us. In Jesus' name, I pray. Amen

# 12

# Humility and Contentment

> "Yea, all of you be subject one to another, and be clothed with humility: for God resisteth the proud, and giveth grace to the humble."
> **1 Peter 5:5**

How do we relate humility to contentment? Think of humility as the Alpha and contentment as the Omega of the Christian life. Humility leads to contentment. There can be no godly contentment without humility. The Spirit of Christ, supernaturally working in the hearts and lives of God's children, produces both.

Pride and discontent are the root and fruit of the life of the world.

The new birth brings us with a new heart to a fresh start ~ the Alpha ~ where He teaches us what He intended in His work of creation. The humility of Christ that enabled Him to give Himself as a sacrifice for us is the same humility His Spirit works in us; so, through us, He can demonstrate humility to the world.

Andrew Murray, in his book, *Humility ~ The Beauty of Holiness*\* stresses the need for us to understand the power of Christ's life and work for and in us.

> "Nothing can avail but that the new nature, in its divine humility, will be revealed in power to take the place of the old. It will become as truly our very nature as the old ever was." *Andrew Murray*

Humility at work in us depends on three things:

> 1. The teaching (revelation from the written word and the Holy Spirit) and Christ's example.
>
> 2. Our convictions, our desires, our prayers, waiting on God in faith for His promise.
>
> 3. The reality of the Spirit of Christ living in us and producing His nature and disposition.

Humility and contentment are divine traits of God's kingdom, and gifts of God's grace to His children. Even as our natural and spiritual births are beyond our doing, humility and contentment are His work alone, and all to His glory.

> "Humility is simply acknowledging the truth of our position as man and yielding to God His place. It is the sense of entire nothingness, which comes when we see how truly God is all, and in which we make way for God to be all. Such humility (the humility of Christ) is not a thing that will come on its own. It must be the object of special desire, prayer, faith, and practice." *Humility*

What Murray says of humility can be said of contentment, as we continue to grow in grace and knowledge of our Lord Jesus Christ (2 Peter 3:18).

When we yield all to Him and live in faith, He provides all that we need. This is the life of contentment.

## Humility and Contentment Work Together

> "Humility is like the lead in the net, which keeps the soul down when it is rising through passion, and contentment is like the cork, which keeps the heart up when it is sinking through discouragement. Contentment is the great support; it is like the beam which bears whatever weight is laid upon it. It is like a rock that breaks the waves." *The Art of Divine Contentment* Thomas Watson

Do we experience divine contentment in Christ? If not, let us look to Him with the conviction of the need for humility. Let us desire in prayer and supplication, in faith through His Word and Spirit, waiting for this "mystery of grace, which teaches us that as we lose ourselves in the overwhelming greatness of redeeming love, humility becomes to us the consummation of everlasting blessedness and adoration." *Humility*

Dear Father, how do we thank you for so great a love that displaces our sin and old life with the graces of the Spirit of Christ in us. Let us be so overwhelmed as to bow in thankfulness and humility for all you have done for us in our creation and our salvation. Make us know the power of your

Spirit to humble us; let us wait patiently with a new heart's desire for all that you have prepared for us. Let us live content and praising you for all things working to your glory, our good, and joy. In Jesus' name, I pray. Amen.

*A Broad Review of Andrew Murray's Humility*

# 13

# The Voice of Contentment

**"I will hear what God the Lord will speak: for he will
speak peace unto his people, and to his saints:
but let them not turn again to folly."
Psalm 85:8**

Whose voice leads you? Infants begin life under the influence of parents and then grow up hearing family and friends. With these familiar voices, the world speaks, and what we hear is written in our minds, hearts, and souls. Except we train our thinking, we become the voice of the world. Processing includes the foundational ideas from our childhood by which we compare all new information. What we see, read, hear, and repeat through the years become our basis and voice of truth.

## The Voice of the Majority

The voice of the majority is one of discontent. We rarely hear the voice of godly contentment except through those who know this voice within them. It is not self-produced or found in the views and the noises of everyday life, but it is the still, small voice of our heavenly Father and Creator. It is the voice in the new heart, new spirit, and new life that is ours in Christ, spoken by the Holy Spirit, kept alive through the reading and hearing of God's Word.

**The Voice of the Oppressor**
The voice of the world is the voice of Satan, the oppressor. We started with two extremes in *Born for Contentment*. Oppression and contentment are the voices God's children hear every day. Either one has the power to drown the other. The voice of contentment must be instructed and practiced if it is to overcome the voice of oppression.

God said, "Let there be light. And there was light." Genesis 1:3 Eve listened to the voice of Satan, the oppressor. He put out the light and silenced God's voice.

After the promise of restoration in Genesis 3:15, God sent His prophets to voice His Words. Moses spoke God's Words to His people.

> "Now, therefore, if you will indeed obey my voice and keep my covenant, you shall be my treasured possession among all peoples, for all the earth is mine; and you shall be to me a kingdom of priests and a holy nation.' These are the words that you shall speak to the people of Israel." Exodus 19: 5-6

> "And all these blessings shall come upon you and overtake you, if you obey the voice of the Lord your God." Deuteronomy 28:2

These and other passages speak of the blessings and contentment that come to those who hear and obey God's voice. Other passages speak of the curses that come to those who do not obey Him.

The writer begins the book of Hebrews with these words;

> "Long ago, at many times and in many ways, God spoke to our fathers by the prophets, but in these last days he has spoken to us by his Son, whom he appointed the heir of all things, through whom also he created the world.
> He is the radiance of the glory of God and the exact imprint of his nature, and he upholds the universe by the word of his power." Hebrews 1:1-3

God's people would not listen to the voice of the prophets. The religious leaders of Jesus' day would not listen to Him, and their voices influenced the people. They were accustomed to the sound of the enemy and did not recognize God's voice through those He sent.

Jesus' voice still speaks today by His Spirit and His Word, and His is the voice of contentment ~ the voice of LIFE. In John 6:63, He said to the people, "The words I have spoken to you are spirit and life."

The voice of oppression says, "More, more. Give me more."

The voice of contentment says, "Christ is enough. He is all I need."

### Repetition
Ministers today must speak warnings against the voice of the world. They are called and ordained for the gospel of truth that brings contentment in a world of oppression. Repetition is what keeps either voice alive.
Do we continually listen and share what the world is saying and doing? Does the world need our voice to speak of its

oppression? Or do we, as those of God's kingdom and family, voice His words, words that inform and encourage others by our contentment, a voice that draws others in obedience to Him?

> "Out of them shall come songs of thanksgiving, and the voices of those who celebrate. I will multiply them, and they shall not be few; I will make them honored, and they shall not be small." Jeremiah 30:19

God, our Father, has given us voices to speak for Him, to praise and honor Him, and to witness of His grace and glory. Are we using our voices to share what He has given us?

> "Because your steadfast love is better than life, my lips will praise you." Psalm 63:3

> "My mouth is filled with your praise, and with your glory all the day." Psalm 71:8

> "My mouth will tell of your righteous acts, of your deeds of salvation all the day, for their number is past my knowledge." Psalm 71:15

Gracious Father, work in us your voice of thanksgiving and praise, from a heart of peace and joy in Christ, our Lord. While others speak the voice of the world, let us respond with the voice of your kingdom. Fill us with your Spirit of contentment that draws others to you. In Jesus' name, I pray. Amen

# 14

# The Price of Contentment

*"You are not your own.
You have been bought with a price."
1 Corinthians 6:19-20).*

For the world, contentment costs nothing more than what money can afford.

The blood of Christ was the means to purchase godly contentment for His followers, born of His Spirit. The love of God was revealed for His children by the death of His Son, purchasing and redeeming us from the bondage of sin and death (Romans 8:2). We are born to a living hope by His abundant mercy and the resurrection of Jesus Christ from the dead; to an inheritance in Him that no one can take away (1 Peter 1:3-4).

It is a legacy that we do not deserve, could not pay for, nor earn, by any good work. Not to be content with the finished work of Christ that assures and provides a pardon from sin and abundant life in Him, is to doubt this gift of His righteousness for us and to live without Him. God so loved us, desired us, sired us and made us His, to lavish His grace, His provisions, His protection, His goodness, His own life for us, in us, and through us.

To His glory, He has shined His light into our hearts to shine through us His grace, mercy, and power. He has given us all things pertaining to life and godliness (2 Peter 1:3) through Christ His Son (Romans 8:32). He has given all for us to reflect His presence, His goodness, and His wealth in and upon us. He has spread abroad His love in our hearts by the Holy Spirit, which He has given us (Romans 5:5).

## Our Response to His Sacrifice and Mercy

In response to His sacrifice and mercy in taking our sin and punishment upon Himself, Paul urges the believers in Romans 12:1-2.

> "I beseech you therefore, brethren, by the mercies of God, that you present your bodies a living sacrifice, holy, acceptable to God, which is your reasonable service. And do not be conformed to this world, but be transformed by the renewing of your mind, that you may prove what is that good and acceptable and perfect will of God." Romans 12:1-2

Here is the reality of a life of contentment, according to His will. His sacrificial death works through us for a sacrificial life devoted to serving Him and others while He is preparing us to share His eternal glory. True contentment cost Jesus His life, and it costs us ours. He denied Himself for us to give us eternal life in Him. To experience this life of contentment, we deny ourselves for Christ's sake. "It is no longer I who live, but Christ who lives in me." Galatians 2:20

## Understanding the Terms of Sacrifice

Eternal life in Christ begins when we are born of His Spirit; by a new heart and spirit we are joined to Christ from that moment. We experience eternal life here, now, and forever. The new birth, faith, and repentance separate us from the world's way of life.

We are no longer our own, conformed to this world, but sanctified, being transformed by the renewing of our minds, and growing in grace and knowledge of Christ until He calls us home to be with Him.

Jesus paid the price for our contentment. Presenting our bodies as a living sacrifice means we have received, understand, accept, and enter into the covenant of life that is ours in His death and resurrection.

Gracious Father, we thank you for your covenant of redemption and grace made with Christ, your Son, before the foundation of the world. We praise you for the work of your Holy Spirit in revealing and fulfilling your covenant with and in us. Enable us to know the power of Christ's resurrection through the continued work of the gospel, bringing us to submission and surrender of all we are, to live in covenant with you, in Christ, now and forever. In Jesus' name, I pray, and thank you. Amen.

# 15

# Patience that Leads to Contentment

**"But let patience have her perfect work,
that ye may be perfect and entire, wanting nothing."
James 1:4**

The title for this chapter came as Jerry and I waited for the nurse to bring his hospital discharge papers late one Monday afternoon. He was admitted as an outpatient early Wednesday morning and discharged as an inpatient late Monday afternoon.

Wednesday, we waited two hours before they took him to insert a stent through an aneurysm in his right leg.

The stent was inserted through a catheter, so after the procedure, we waited while they applied pressure to stop the bleeding. Jerry had to stay overnight to be sure there would be no more bleeding.

Thursday, we waited for the results of an ultrasound that showed the artery had not sealed and for the news that Jerry would need major surgery to seal the artery.

Then we waited for the results of an EKG and ultrasound of his heart to determine if he could endure the surgery.

Friday, we waited for the outcome of the surgery.

Saturday and Sunday, we stayed while a wound vac suctioned drainage from the four-inch incision.

Monday, we waited until the vascular surgeon removed the wound vac. At home, we waited for Jerry's healing and our strength to return so that we could continue to serve the Lord.

We have indeed experienced many blessings every day, as the Lord continues to show us His mercy and grace. It is in these difficult times that He continues to grow us in grace and knowledge of our Lord Jesus Christ.

Before I began this chapter, my thoughts were centered on how to describe the true Christian life. The words, faithful, obedient, and steadfast, were a few that came to mind. Patience is not always the first that we think of, but if we look to the last book of God's Word, we find Revelation 13:10 and 14:12 (KJV) both speak of "the patience of the saints." The English Standard Version translates patience as endurance.

> "If anyone is to be taken captive, to captivity he goes; if anyone is to be slain with the sword, with the sword must he be slain. Here is a call for the endurance and faith of the saints."

When I think of waiting in the circumstances of this life, it in no way compares to the terms of "taken captive" or "slain with the sword." In Revelation 14:12-13, we find again the word endurance related to faithfulness and faith of the saints in Jesus.

> "Here is a call for the endurance of the saints, those who keep the commandments of God and their faith in Jesus.

## Patience that Leads to Contentment

> And I heard a voice from heaven saying, "Write this: Blessed are the dead who die in the Lord from now on." "Blessed indeed," says the Spirit, "that they may rest from their labors, for their deeds follow them!"

It is incredible what the Lord does during our times of adversity.

Waiting is linked to patiently enduring whatever He has planned for us, working all things for our good, as He has predestined us to be conformed to the image of Christ (Romans 8:28-29) even as He is faithful to us in all that He is and does.

Three main thoughts came during those six days in the hospital (this is our third visit since it opened three years ago):

1. God, our Father, is always faithful, even when we are not.
2. He promises to complete the work He has begun in us and provides blessings in situations we would rather avoid (Philippians 1:6).
3. We mature when we endure.

Contentment was the only sense that I experienced as we waited for Jerry's discharge papers Monday afternoon, the fruit of the Lord's working in my heart during those six days.

Dear Father, we thank you for continuing to fill us with your grace, wrapping us in your glory, so that you will not fail to bring us through this life in Christ, even as you are preparing us for your eternal glory.

We praise you that you never fail, always able to hold us, strengthen is, and grow us as your children. Fill us with your Spirit and through us, witness to others of your goodness. In Jesus' name, I thank you and praise you. Amen.

# 16

# The Flow of Contentment

**"out of his heart will flow rivers of living water."**
**John 7:38 ESV**

Contentment is woven into God's kingdom, experienced by His people as we live daily by the filling of His Holy Spirit. Other chapters brought us to know the legacy that is ours and to keep us content in His kingdom.

In this chapter, we want to look at the difference in what God creates ~ a world of contentment ~ and what man creates.

When we look at God's creation, we see a flow man can never create or discern. Between the sky and the earth, there is a connection. We cannot determine where one ends, and the other begins.

**No Corners**
Notice that there are no corners and nothing to stop the flow. God has planned for the present heavens and earth to be replaced by a new heaven and earth where His people will be part of the new creation (2 Peter 3:10-14).

According to His plan and power, in His timing, He will show His presence and authority over all things.

**Continual Light**
At different times, darkness covers parts of the earth. On another side of the earth, the light of the sun continues to shine, even casting its reflection on the moon as a reminder of God's presence with us. So, too, the light in our hearts continues to flow so that we are content with His presence and power at all times in our lives (2 Corinthians 4:6-7).

**Water**
Water flows from heaven to the earth, in the springs, the streams, the waterfalls, the rivers, and the ocean. So, too, the Spirit of the Lord continues to fill us with the life of Christ.

Plants and trees grow upward and outward, landscaping the terrain in beauty from one hillside and mountain to another, even as they reach to and praise the Creator.

So, too, as the fruit of the Spirit in us brings us in unity with each other, we praise our heavenly Father and our Lord (Galatians 5:22-23).

None of God's creation has anything to hide, so we see all things living openly and peacefully, uninhibited by pride and sin. They are content to be a part of the flow, producing what the Creator planned for each one. We, too, are content when we experience the flow of the Spirit of the Lord, creating what He desires in each of us. He frees us from pride to live in humility as a witness of His work in and through us.

### Animals
Animals in their natural habitats are not cornered but live by the cycles of each day, as the Lord feeds them. (Psalm 145:15-16); even the birds of the air and the fish of the sea (Psalm 8:8

### Life and Death
Even in His creation, He planned for the flow of life and death. He created us to reflect His image in the middle of it all.

As we consider His relationship with all of His creation, we can live in the state of contentment. Believing whatever is happening in our own lives, personally, or the world as a whole, He is in the flow, carrying all things throughout eternity, now and forever, for His glory, our good, and our joy.

Our Father in heaven; continually fill us with your Spirit. Make us know the fullness of Christ and the contentment that only you can give. Move us in the flow of your power through this world of chaos and draw others to you. In Jesus' name, I pray, I thank you, and praise you. Amen.]

# 17

# Contentment vs. Anxiety

**"Be anxious for nothing, but in everything by prayer
and supplication, with thanksgiving,
let your requests be made known to God;"
Philippians 4:6**

It took a while for me to write this chapter, It was not because I was at my task of caring for Jerry. It was not because there are not enough hours in the day to witness the Lord's goodness ~ this is the reason I write. Titles come so very quickly, but the meat is not always simple to come by. We long to publish the truths of the Father's kingdom, but the process is better when it comes by experience.

A person who grows up in an environment of anxiety can be stamped for life. But, when we encounter Christ and learn of Him, we are born of and sealed with His Spirit of promise, sanctified, and set apart for His use.

Jacob wrestled with the angel of the Lord. We, too, struggle in our own way for the promises that are ours in Him.

Wrestling is the work of the Holy Spirit within us, bringing us to know and claim the promises through God's Word. Working through life with the two-edged sword, we destroy the strongholds in our lives (2 Corinthians 10:4-5).

There is as much difference between contentment and anxiety as between day and night. The difference is as light and darkness; as good and evil. And each has its different connotations. I could say more of the books written, messages spoken, and songs I have sung, but here I speak simply of how the Lord brings us from the anxiety of this life to contentment in Him.

### The Source and the Fruit

Anxiety is the abnormal attitude of human beings; the seed thought of every man, flowing from the spring of unbelief.

"O, ye of little faith."

"Yes, Lord, I hear you. I recognize your voice. I acknowledge my lack of faith."

"Why do you doubt?"

"I have no excuse. My thoughts carry me where I do not want to go. They seem to have a power of their own."

"Have I not proven that I love you and can provide all that you need?"

"Yes, Lord, I am guilty of forgetting you and your goodness. When my thoughts wander from you in times of difficulty, I am carried away by the moment. I am still learning to be content in every circumstance. I confess my sin and ask that your Spirit keep me in your Word, always to remember your promises. Let me not dwell on the things of the world, and the power of the enemy. But let your Word be the source of my thoughts, to do its work. Restore unto me the joy of thy salvation and the contentment that is mine in you.

Bear in and through me the fruit of your Spirit of love, joy, peace, patience, kindness, goodness, faithfulness, gentleness, temperance, the fruit of holiness, righteousness, truth, grace, and humility. Fill me with your fullness, so there is no room for doubt or fear, but only thoughts of you, your grace, and your glory." In Jesus' name, I pray. Amen.

# 18

# Peace and Contentment

**"My people will dwell in a peaceful habitation,
In secure dwellings, and in quiet resting places,"
Isaiah 32:18**

Who today, can write of peace and contentment, first-hand? In seeking to share what I have discovered from God's Word, this may have been the chapter I needed the most. It is one thing to write what I have learned, second-hand, but quite different to share from experience. I do not do the subject of peace justice. I cannot cover it all. So, I pray the Lord's blessings for what we offer here.

I know the peace that is "the fruit of the Spirit" of God (Galatians 5:22). I can share no other peace than what God has given me through His Son, Jesus Christ (Romans 5:1). I have experienced His peace, but I have many times been lacking, not because I do not have peace, but because it is not a natural trait. This peace is proven while I live amid chaos.

Here, we will pose some questions and attempt to answer from the Word of the Lord.

How do peace and contentment relate to each other? There is no Biblical reference that combines these two. Since we have written many other chapters on the subject of contentment, we will document what we know of peace, seeing that the two are similar and understanding that one compliments the other. If we have the peace of God through His Son, Jesus Christ, we will be content in His peace.

**The Source of Peace**
The question is not "what" but "where and who is the source of peace?" Peace comes from the Lord, our God, who created all things for peace in His kingdom.

He is still the source and the giver of His peace.

> "The Lord lift up his countenance upon thee, and give thee peace." Numbers 6:26

> "The Lord will give strength unto his people; the Lord will bless his people with peace." Psalm 29:11

We are "led forth with peace." Isaiah 55:12

He has "made a covenant of peace, an everlasting covenant with His people." Ezekiel 37:26

> "He keeps in perfect peace those whose mind is stayed on Him and trusts in Him." Isaiah 26:3

> "Lord, thou wilt ordain peace for us: for thou also hast wrought all our works in us. Isaiah 26:12

He promises His people a peaceable habitation, and in sure dwellings, and in quiet resting places; Isaiah 32:18

Peace is associated with His light. Isaiah 45:7

He creates "the fruit of the lips; 'Peace.'" Isaiah 57:19

He extends peace to His people "like a river," Isaiah 66:12

> "For I know the thoughts that I think toward you, saith the Lord, thoughts of peace, and not of evil, to give you an expected end." Jeremiah 29:11

He reveals his "abundance of peace and truth." Jeremiah 33:6

## HE IS THE GOD OF PEACE

> "For God is not the author of confusion, but of peace." 1 Corinthians 14:33

In letters to the early churches, the apostle Paul included greetings from the God of peace Romans 15:33, Romans 16:20, 2 Thessalonians 3:16
He is "the God of hope that fills believers with joy and peace." Romans 15:13

As the God of peace, He established the everlasting covenant through Christ (Hebrews 13:20), sanctifies and preserves His people until Christ returns (1 Thessalonians 5:23).

## PEACE OF GOD

The peace of God "rules in our hearts," Colossians 3:15

> "And the peace of God, which passeth all understanding, shall keep your hearts and minds through Christ Jesus." Philippians 4:7

## PEACE FROM GOD

Paul spoke of "grace and peace from God our Father, and the Lord Jesus Christ to the saints and brethren" in Romans 1:7, Colossians 1:2, 1 Corinthians 1:3, 2 Corinthians 1:2, Galatians 1:3, Ephesians 1:2, 2 Thessalonians 1:2, Titus 1:4, Philemon 1:3.

John spoke of "grace, mercy, and peace, in truth and love." 2 John 1:3

## PEACE WITH GOD

There is only one reference to peace with God, which comes by faith through our Lord Jesus Christ.

> "Therefore being justified by faith, we have peace with God through our Lord Jesus Christ:" Romans 5:1

## RIGHTEOUSNESS AND PEACE

There are many references that associate peace with righteousness. The most familiar may be found in Romans.

# Peace and Contentment

"For the kingdom of God is not meat and drink; but righteousness, and peace, and joy in the Holy Ghost." Romans 14:17

The Psalmist speaks of the peace that comes by righteousness. Psalm 72:3

"Righteousness and peace have kissed each other." Psalm 85:10

"the righteous flourish; with abundance of peace." Psalm 72:7

"And the work of righteousness shall be peace; and the effect of righteousness quietness and assurance forever." Isaiah 32:17

And "the fruit of righteousness is sown in peace of them that make peace." James 3:18

The writer of Hebrews 12:11 says that "chastening yields the peaceable fruit of righteousness unto them which are exercised thereby."

Paul instructs Timothy to "follow righteousness, faith, charity, peace, with them that call on the Lord out of a pure heart" (2 Timothy 2:22).

## WISDOM AND PEACE
Peace is the result of wisdom.

"For length of days, and long life, and peace, shall they add to thee." Proverbs 3:2

"Her ways are ways of pleasantness, and all her paths are peace." Proverbs 3:17

"The wisdom that is from above is first pure, then peaceable," James 3:17

## GOSPEL OF PEACE
Paul speaks of "our feet shod with the preparation of the gospel of peace." Ephesians 6:15 and "the feet of them that preach the gospel of peace! Romans 10:15

## GOD'S LAW AND PEACE
Those who love God's law have "great peace: and nothing shall offend them." Psalm 119:165

Great peace comes from the Lord as He teaches us. Isaiah 54:13

Gracious Father of grace and peace, we thank you for giving us your Son that we may come to you in His peace; that we may live in peace with you and Him through the power of your Holy Spirit. Fill us with your Spirit, that we may live in this peace, content with whatever you have chosen for us as you prepare us for your glory. In Jesus' name, I pray. Amen.

## 19

# A Conclusive Contentment

**"But the scripture hath concluded all under sin,
that the promise by faith of Jesus Christ
might be given to them that believe."
Galatians 3:22**

As I searched for cover images, I came across some referring to "CONTENT." Finding these images reiterated the truth of what it means to experience the state of contentment. Content relates to the interior ~ what others cannot see. The kernel that begins in our mind takes root then springs forward and outward so that we share what we have inside.

Former chapters in this book show us the source and the means of contentment. They relate to the inner life centered in Christ and Christ living His life in us. It is the content of Christ within that makes us content. The promise of eternal life in Christ sustains and matures our faith and our contentment through this life. As we conclude our thoughts on the reality of Godly Contentment, we do so with the assurance that all life is given through Jesus Christ. He is content to dwell with us and lead us through this life, preparing us for eternity with Him.

We live each day in the light of what He has promised, not just for today, but for eternity.

As our faith grows, our contentment in Him will flourish, and our witness will be more evident to those around us. His grace and His glory will draw others to Him.

Let us review the three main points of our treatise on contentment.

> 1. Godly contentment is supernatural, possible only for God's people.
> 2. It is the result of a relationship between God, our heavenly Father, and His children.
> 3. He teaches and shows us how He works it in us.

As we continue to experience the work of His Holy Spirit guiding us through His Word, our delight in our Lord will grow We will be settled and able to stand in the truth of His grace. His contentment is worth our prayers, our study and meditation, desiring with all our heart, and waiting for Him to work this gift of grace within us.

Dear Heavenly Father, thank you for taking us in hand to bring us from the state of oppression to the state of contentment through your plan of redemption in Jesus, your Son. We praise you for such a great love that overwhelms us and brings us in your blessedness in the Spirit of Christ ~ to a life of worship and adoration now and for eternity. Continue to lead us in this divine contentment to share your grace with others; for your glory and our joy. In Jesus' name I pray. Amen.

# From the Author

Ten years after thinking my life was coming to an end, God is still working to reveal Himself to me. In my eightieth year, the new heart He gave me twenty-seven years ago is continually filled and overflowing with His grace. It is through the power of His will that He has enabled me to live joyfully as a caregiver for members of our family: my father with cancer, my grandchildren, my mother with dementia, and my husband for thirteen years, who was an amputee with heart disease and diabetes. There is no better life than that of serving the Master by serving others.

We began writing these beautiful things of His kingdom to provide a legacy for our grandchildren. From file boxes to computer documents, we have been creating an archive by publishing our books since 2016, so these will be available to future generations. They are here for anyone who wants to read of how the Lord works in the hearts and lives of His people as He is preparing us to share His eternal glory. Profits from sales of our books are designated for missions and charity.

Fran

"For the Lord is good, His mercy is everlasting, and His truth endures to all generations." Psalm 100:5

> **FREE eBook**
> *FIRST THINGS That Last FOREVER*
>
> Other books by Fran Rogers on Amazon.com.

Blog: godsgracegodsglory.com
Facebook: Father and Family Books
Contact: f.rogers@bellsouth.net

**Little Books About the Magnitude of God** *(Published\*)*

*\*FIRST THINGS That Last FOREVER*
*\*TWO FULL PLATES ~ Learning to be a Caregiver*
*\*The Garden of GOD'S WORD~ The Purpose and Delight of BIBLE STUDY*
*\*The LITTLE BOAT and other Short Stories of GOD'S GRACE*
*\*GOD Is Our Goal*
*Notes on Paul's Letter to the Romans*
*Legacy of the Seven Psalms + One*
*God's Grace ~ God's Glory*

**Series What the Holy Bible Says**

*\*What the Holy BIBLE Says About LIGHT*
*\*What the Holy BIBLE Says About the WORD of GOD*
*What the Holy BIBLE Says About LIFE*

**Other Books**
*\*Prayers That Bring the House Down*
*\*One Month to Live ~ A Father's Last Words*
*\*A Broad Review of Andrew Murray's Humility"*
*\*Child Keeping ~ God's Blessing to Parents*
*\*Beyond a mere Christianity*
*Waiting is Not a Game ~ Articles of Faith*
*The Master Gardener and other Poems of GOD'S GRACE*

www.ingramcontent.com/pod-product-compliance
Lightning Source LLC
Chambersburg PA
CBHW031455040426
42444CB00007B/1114